ISBN: 9781764274586

First Edition

Pippa Bird

Grieving Goanna

One sunny day in the Australian bush, Goldie the goanna climbed a nearby tree to offer her friend a wander down to the creek.

But her friend wasn't there.

Goldie looked in her friend's other favourite spot, but he wasn't there either.

"Where are you, Gordon?"

Goldie climbed down from the trees
and lay in the dirt against a rock,
feeling the warmth but not the joy.

She missed her friend, but wasn't
quite sure of this new feeling.

Eddie waddled by. Noticing Goldie's sadness, he gently approached her.

"Hello Goldie," Eddie started softly, "You seem quite down. Is everything okay?"

Goldie sniffled, "I cannot find my friend Gordon. I looked in the only two places that I ever find him, and he's not there."

"Why did he leave me, Eddie?"

"Well, I'm not sure, Goldie," the echidna thought for a moment, "Did he tell you he was leaving?"

"No. He told me he felt rather tired lately. More tired than usual. I suggested he rest his body, but he said his mind was tired too."

"Oh, I see," started Eddie, "Your friend, Gordon, was he much older than you?"

"Twice my age," Goldie replied,
"But what does that matter?"

"It matters a great
deal, Goldie."

"Often, goannas like yourself, venture off to seek a quiet, hidden place to begin their forever sleep."

Goldie's brow furrowed, "Forever sleep? But couldn't I wake him up to play, if I found him?"

"No, dear goanna. Gordon's time on earth has finished. You will only see him in your memories, your dreams. And those you must cherish."

Tears welled in Goldie's eyes. Her heart felt heavier than ever before.

She curled up onto the bush floor
and remained silent for a long while.

Tears welled in Eddie's eyes as he remained by her
side. He perched himself against a nearby tree, giving
Goldie a little space until she was ready to talk.

After some time, the goanna
sighed, but remained still.
Eddie waited patiently.

"This feeling. What is it? I don't like
it. How do I feel better, Eddie?"

The echidna sighed
before speaking, "Grief."

"What you feel, Goldie, is grief. It
hurts more than one hundred harsh
winter days, or twice as many drought-
stricken weeks."

"It hurts more than a bee sting,
or my spine in your paw. It is
heavy. And it lingers."

"It sounds horrible.
How do I feel better?"

"Talking about it may help.
Remembering Gordon,
and the things about him
that made you happy,"
Eddie replied.

Goldie climbed to her feet but didn't utter a word.

"You can honour him in silence too, Goldie, but it's important to let yourself feel these emotions," said Eddie.

"We can do it together."

In a nearby tree, Kiya couldn't help but overhear Goldie and Eddie's conversation.

Kiya started climbing down from her tree, "I'm here for you too, Goldie."

"Sometimes, sharing your feelings with friends can make the load a little lighter."

With the support of her friends, Goldie began to open up about her feelings. She talked about the happy memories she had with Gordon and how much she missed him.

Eddie and Kiya listened patiently, offering comfort and understanding while holding space for Goldie's emotions.

Days later, and Goldie found solace in the presence of her friends. One day, Eddie had an idea.

"Let's create a memorial to honour Gordon," he suggested.

Eddie began scratching at the
earth beneath a log.

Kiya and Goldie watched as
he gathered several twigs to
place beneath the log.

Goldie found a number of pebbles
and driftwood on the edge of the
creek.

She collected them in a small pile.

Kiya found a large field of
yellow dandelions blooms.

She gently gathered a bundle,
careful not to stir the bees.

The three of them began to shape a small memorial - arranging driftwood and stones, leaves and flowers.

Together they created a place to remember Gordon. A place Goldie could visit when she missed her friend.

Goldie returned often. Not
every day. Just when the
wind stirred the canopy in a
certain way.

Or when the sun
warmed the rocks
like it used to.

She didn't forget Gordon. She didn't try to. Goldie felt
her feelings, embracing the loss by remembering the
happiest moments she had with him.

The ache soon softened, like water smoothing stone.
She was patient with the process.

In the hush of the bushland, among creatures who came and went, Goldie found a rhythm again.

Not the same. But steady. Understanding the process of grief certainly helped her heart heal a little more each day.

Calm Kangaroo series by Pippa Bird. Available on Amazon.

Calm Kangaroo
Mindfulness Alphabet
Written & Illustrated by Pippa Bird

Quiet Quokka
Written & Illustrated by Pippa Bird

Positive Platypus
Soula's Self-image
Written & Illustrated by Pippa Bird

Co-regulating Koala
Lost and Found
Written & Illustrated by Pippa Bird

Unwind with Calm Kangaroo
Written & Illustrated by Pippa Bird

Positive Platypus
Posy's Special Find
Written & Illustrated by Pippa Bird

Co-regulating Koala
Tumbling Tower
Written & Illustrated by Pippa Bird

Co-regulating Koala
The Loud Crack
Written & Illustrated by Pippa Bird

Wobbly Roo
Pippa Bird

Logical Lyrebird
Pippa Bird

Hop by Hop
A Gentle Approach to Autism Acceptance
Pippa Bird

Hop, Skip, Rest
A Gentle Approach to Understanding ADHD
Pippa Bird

Elated Emu
Pippa Bird

Corroborate Cockatoo
Pippa Bird

Kind Kookaburra
Pippa Bird

Timely Tarantula
Pippa Bird

Nonsense Numbat
Pippa Bird

Polite Python
Pippa Bird

Bully Bilby
Pippa Bird

Empathetic Echidna
Pippa Bird

About the Author
Pippa Bird is a former Mental Health Therapist in Private Practice Alula Blu Counselling Services, in regional NSW

Pippa holds a Bachelor in Psychology, a Diploma in Counselling, and a Diploma in Graphic Design, with a primary focus on illustration.

Calm Kangaroo

CALM KANGAROO is a backronym title for a children's mental and emotional well-being program. An initiative designed to educate children about mental health and foster a learning journey of emotional intelligence, resilience and cultivate an open mind through the benefits of reading well-being books, leading to the most important discussions and ideas.

CALM KANGAROO focuses on Curating, Advocating & Leading Mindfulness, & its mission to Kindle Awareness, Nurture Growth, Amplify Resilience, & Orchestrate Open-minds.